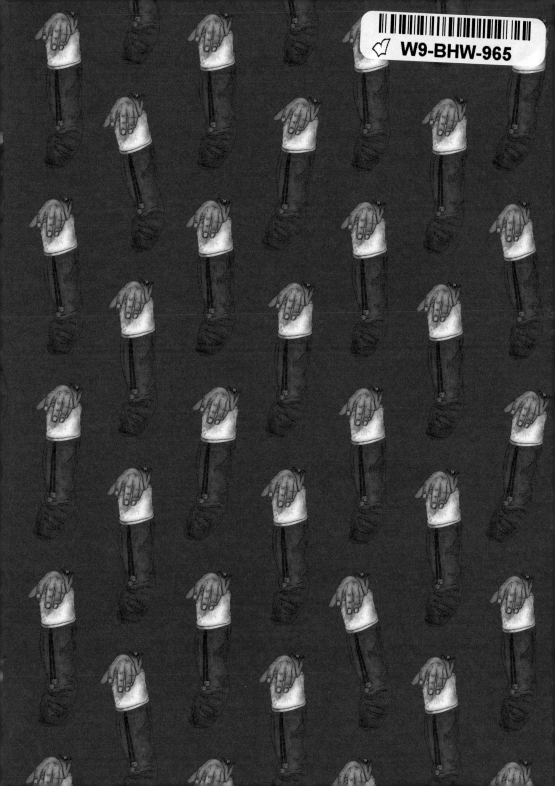

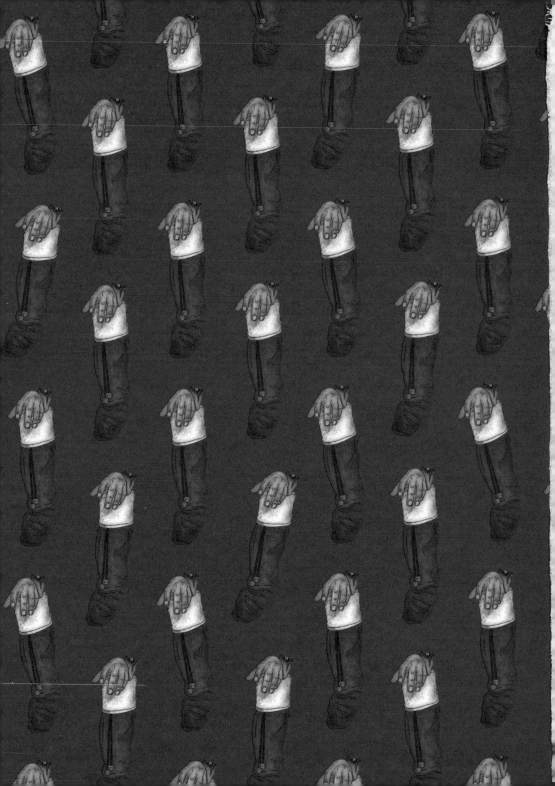

THE
Zombie Night
Before Christmas

by Clement C. Moore and H. Parker Kelley
Illustrations by Dominic Mylroie

CIDER MILL PRESS

BOOK
PUBLISHERS

Kennebunkport, Maine

13-Digit ISBN: 978-1-60433-202-5
10-Digit ISBN: 1-60433-202-6

This book may be ordered by mail from the publisher.
Please include $2.95 for postage and handling.
Please support your local bookseller first!

Books published by Cider Mill Press Book Publishers are available at special discounts for
bulk purchases in the United States by corporations, institutions, and other organizations.
For more information, please contact the publisher.

Cider Mill Press Book Publishers
"Where good books are ready for press"
12 Port Farm Road
Kennebunkport, Maine 04046

Visit us on the Web!
www.cidermillpress.com

Design by Alicia Freile, Tango Media
Printed in China

1 2 3 4 5 6 7 8 9 0
First Edition

To all our friends, living, dead, and living dead.

'Twas the night before Christmas,
when all through the house
Not a zombie was stirring,
not even a mouse;

The stockings were hung
by the chimney with care,
In hopes that St. Nicholas
soon would be there;

The children were nestled
all snug in their beds,
While visions of body parts
danced in their heads;

And mama in her 'kerchief
and I in my cap,
Had just settled our brains
for a long winter's nap,

When out on the lawn
there arose such a clatter,
I sprang from the dead
to see what was the matter.

Away to the window
I limped in a flash,
Tore open the shutters
and gnawed on the sash.

The moon on the breast
of the new-fallen snow
Gave a lustre of bone-white
to objects below,

When, what to my deadening
eyes should appear,
But a miniature sleigh,
and eight yummy reindeer,

With a little old driver,
so lively and quick,
I knew in a moment
I must bite St. Nick.

More rapid than eagles
his coursers they came,
And he whistled, and shouted,
and called them by name;

"Now Dasher! now, Dancer!
now, Prancer and Vixen!
On, Comet! on Cupid!
on, Donder and Blitzen!

To the top of the porch!
to the top of the wall!
Now dash away! dash away!
dash away all!"

As dry leaves that before
the wild hurricane fly,
When they meet with an obstacle,
mount to the sky,

So up to the house-top
the coursers they flew,
With the sleigh full of toys,
and St. Nicholas too.

And then, in a twinkling,
I heard on the roof
The prancing and pawing
of each little hoof.

As I drew in my hand,
and was turning around,
Down the chimney St. Nicholas
came with a bound.

He was dressed all in fur,
from his head to his foot,
And his clothes were all tarnished
with ashes and soot;

A bundle of toys
he had flung on his back,
And he looked like a peddler
unprepared for attack.

His eyes—how they twinkled!
his dimples how merry!
His cheeks were like roses,
his nose like a cherry!

His droll little mouth
was drawn up like a bow,
And the beard on his chin
was as white as the snow;

The stump of his head
I held tight in my teeth,
And the blood it encircled
his head like a wreath;

He had a broad face
and a little round belly,
That bled, when he laughed,
like a bowl of red jelly!

He was chubby and plump,
a right jolly old elf,
And I chomped when I saw him,
in spite of myself;

A blink of his eyes
and twist of his head,
Soon let me know
he was now living dead;

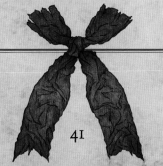

He spoke not a word,
but went straight to his work,
And filled all the stockings;
then turned with a jerk,

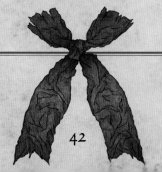

And laying a finger
aside of his nose,
And giving a nod,
up the chimney he rose;

He sprang to his sleigh,
to his team gave a whistle,
And away they all flew
like the down of a thistle.

But I heard him exclaim,
ere he drove out of sight,

ZOMBIE CHRISTMAS
TO ALL, AND TO ALL
A GOOD NIGHT!"

ABOUT CIDER MILL PRESS BOOK PUBLISHERS

Good ideas ripen with time. From seed to harvest,
Cider Mill Press brings fine reading, information,
and entertainment together between the covers of
its creatively crafted books. Our Cider Mill bears
fruit twice a year, publishing a new crop
of titles each spring and fall.

Visit us on the web at
www.cidermillpress.com
or write to us at
12 Port Farm Road
Kennebunkport, Maine 04046